JESUS WEPT

BRUCE MARCHIANO

HOWARD
PUBLISHING CO.

Our purpose at Howard Publishing is to:

• *Increase faith* in the hearts of growing Christians

• *Inspire holiness* in the lives of believers

• *Instill hope* in the hearts of struggling people everywhere

Because He's coming again!

DEDICATION

To my pastor, Scott Bauer, in his memory
I miss you, Scott.
As a shepherd you led me like Jesus—
as a man you called me Friend.
Rest assured, dear Brother,
for through me and the many others
you poured yourself into,

your ministry lives on!

CONTENTS

CONTENTS

ACKNOWLEDGMENTS

The grace of our God is so big, and I just thank Him for leading me so specifically to Howard Publishing . . .

Thank you John, Denny, Philis, and company for your constant support, genuine care, and your willingness to step "out of the box" so that people would know the heart of God.

Thank you, also, to Mary Ann Jeffries whose encouragement is the reason this book exists; to Gesina, who believes in me beyond what I can understand; and to the many people across the world, most of whom I've never met, who selflessly and privately carry me in prayer . . . *Thank you!*

"LET US FIX OUR EYES ON JESUS"

As many of you may know, several years ago I had the remarkable privilege of portraying Jesus on film. The movie is called *The Gospel of Matthew,* and the incredible thing about it is, that's exactly what the movie is—word for word, the Gospel of Matthew. As an actor I had to memorize Jesus' every word and strive to understand His heart like never before. The only word to describe that time in my life is *extraordinary.*

But that's not the experience I want to focus on in this introduction to *Jesus Wept.* Rather, it's something that happened years later—in fact, just a few months ago.

Consider him . . . so that you will not grow weary and lose heart.

I was scheduled to speak at a gathering of maybe two thousand people. When I walked into the auditorium, the music had already begun, and I could tell the evening was going to be a great time of celebrating Jesus.

Right away something on the stage caught my eye. There, propped on an easel along the right side of the platform, was a huge painting—a montage of three images of Jesus, two of which were obviously based on scenes from *The Gospel of Matthew*.

Now, I've seen my own face in paintings of Jesus before. As you might imagine, it feels a little funny. I'm humbled and honored that what I did on film means so much to some people that they would actually paint it. But seeing one of those paintings, especially when it's big—some have been huge!—kind of makes me want to crawl under a table.

The two images from the movie were of Jesus bloodied and hanging on the cross and Jesus weeping over a blind beggar's shoulder, holding him tight against His chest, just weeping and weeping. This second image brought back one of my favorite memories of the entire filming—a favorite because in that scene, Jesus was revealed to me like I'd never understood Him before.

INTRODUCTION

*You will . . . find me when you
seek me with all your heart.*

I will never forget it. We were filming in rural Morocco, and the man who played the blind beggar really was a blind beggar. Sparing you all the pre-scene details, the director called, "Action!" and the filming began. Suddenly I found myself down in the dirt with this guy,

> face to face
> > close up
> > > eye to eye

just as Jesus undoubtedly was when the encounter really took place two thousand years ago.

As the scene progressed, I was so overwhelmed with this man's brokenness that I started to cry and cry. My heart shattered, and all I could do was cry.

But far beyond my own feelings, what really hit me was Jesus' heartbreak over him—the depth of Jesus' compassion for this man and how desperately Jesus must love him. I tell you, I knew about Jesus' love for people in pain before that day, but I never really "got it" until that moment.

For the very first time, with every tear that I cried as I knelt in that Moroccan sand, I understood that Jesus was crying a thousand more. He loves that man so much—so desperately . . .

Streams of tears flow from my eyes because my people are destroyed.

And I just broke completely. I pulled the guy into my arms, and long after the camera stopped rolling, I cried and cried and cried. You could have heard a pin drop; the cast and crew were frozen. I will never forget what one cast member told me while watching the footage later: "I've known Jesus a long time, but I don't think I ever really *knew* Him until now."

Flash forward. There I was, about to speak to the crowd, and I saw that "revelation moment" immortalized in a painting sitting to the right of the stage. The memories flooded back to me—the memory of the experience and the memory of discovering *who Jesus truly is* within it.

Immediately after the service, I asked around and discovered that the artist was there at the gathering. We met and hugged. She said she was so excited to meet me. Then she began to tell me why she had painted that painting and why she'd chosen those specific images for her montage. And I tell you, as she explained her reasons for painting the scene of Jesus and the blind man, I was overwhelmed all over again.

This woman, this artist, said that some time ago she had suffered a brutal and violent rape. (Forgive me for being so blunt, but the only way I know to say it is to just say it.) I didn't learn the particulars, and I was at least smart enough not to ask. Suffice it to say, it was a horrific tragedy. I have to guess that unless you've been through such a thing, you can't imagine it. And my being a guy especially— in a million years I'm sure I couldn't begin to understand the depths of the nightmare this woman experienced.

She told me about the pain and the trauma, the shame and the fear, and her desperate attempts to "climb free" of it all. Then someone introduced her to *The Gospel of Matthew,* and after discovering Jesus in all His compassionate reality, she was set free. And today she stands completely free!

No more shame

    no more nightmares

        no more fear

—just completely free, free, free! Oh, praise the name of Jesus! Isn't He something? I love it!

Here's the thing she told me: "Bruce, I've known Jesus since I was a little girl, but I didn't know He cried over my pain. I didn't know His heart broke even more than mine when I suffered. He was there that night, Bruce, weeping and weeping for what was happening to me. I never knew that. I was just so angry at Him for what happened. But He didn't cause it. In fact, it tore Him up. I just never knew before . . ."

Somehow, watching that scene with the blind beggar, this woman learned what I learned in reenacting it:

Jesus' compassion

    His heartbreak

        His love

—the breathtaking depth of it all—in the midst of our crises. And it healed her soul.

Then she explained about the crucifixion image. She said this picture expressed her realization that as much as she had suffered, Jesus suffered far more. He carried the weight of her pain, the horror of the rape, on His shoulders that day. He suffered through it all and then some. She realized that she was not alone in her pain—that Jesus knew pain too. He knew *her* pain. And once again, the realization healed her soul.

He was pierced . . . he was crushed . . .
the punishment that brought us peace was upon him.

The act of painting helped solidify and document her healing process. With each stroke, she immersed herself more deeply in Jesus' compassion and love for her—and her soul was healed even more.

It is that compassion—those tears that Jesus weeps over our sorrow and tears, our losses and grief, our pain and brokenness; it is His pain in the midst of our pain—your pain, my pain—*that's* what *Jesus Wept* is all about. That's why I took the time to write it, and hopefully you'll take the time to read it. Because when we immerse ourselves in an understanding of the love and compassion of Jesus—of who He truly is in the reality and fullness of His Person—when we "consider him," as Hebrews 12:3 says, we "will not grow weary and lose heart," and our souls will be healed. Oh, how He longs to reach in and heal our souls!

Every one of us remembers the events of September 11, 2001, all too well. One could easily call it "the tragedy of all tragedies," if I may use that phrase—fully sensitive to the fact that day in and day out, as people in a broken world, we suffer all sorts of tragedies. That day just seemed like a whole lot more. And I don't think many people would argue with me, considering the sheer magnitude of the destruction and the compound layers of agony—the lives upon lives that were snagged in the grip of that horror; the lives upon lives that are still being pieced back together because of that terror.

There's just no minimizing September 11. May I say to those of us who weren't directly affected by losing family or friends: We can say we understand all day long, but I promise you, there's just no way we can ever really know what others have gone through. And may I say to those of you who did lose loved ones that day: I'm so, so sorry. I know these are only empty words, but they're all I have. I'm just so, so sorry.

If you don't mind, because that day is so universally etched in our collective hearts and minds, I'd like to refer to it occasionally in the pages that follow. I'd like to talk about it symbolically, as a kind of metaphor representing

all our losses
all our heartaches
all our tragedies

—all our crises in life in general. There are men and women who lost their spouses on September 11, and that's so beyond tragedy. But there are men and women who have lost their spouses on other days as well; and in the privacy of their hearts, it is no less a tragedy. They, too, need to understand what my artist friend came to understand—*the heart of Jesus in the middle of it all.*

This isn't a book about September 11; rather, it's a book about Jesus and His heart in the middle of all our "September 11s."

All of us so desperately need Jesus. We need a deep, deep understanding of His heart and His love for us, and we need to know that He weeps right along with us, that He mourns for our losses. They tear holes in His heart just as they tear holes in ours—even more so.

We so desperately need to know that He's not just sitting somewhere up there, far removed, busy being God, harboring the condescending attitude, "I've given you My Word, so get over it." We need to know that He isn't flinging lightning bolts at our lives—putting us through hellish things as He mockingly says, "I'm the Potter and you're the clay, so get happy."

We so desperately need to know *the truth* of His heart—

the softness
  the compassion
    the brokenness

He feels from His own pain and because of ours.

Jesus Wept is a focus on Jesus. It is a journey into His heart. It is a portrait of Jesus in the midst of our pain—how He feels, how He's affected, what our pain means to Him, what it does to His heart. So come, "consider him," as the Scripture says. Consider Jesus in the face of whatever anguish or struggle you're going through right now, "so that you will not grow weary and lose heart."

May I pray?

Lord, I don't know this one who is reading these words, but You do. You know it all, Lord—

> *every struggle and hardship*
> > *every grief and loss*
> > > *every hunger and heartache.*

O Lord, when we look at our circumstances, there's so much we can't understand. But whatever is happening in our lives, Lord, we so need You. We need rest for our souls—and that rest is You.

Your desire is simple, Your promise sure: "Come to Me, My child, and you will find rest for your soul."

So through these words that follow, Lord, bless this reader. Draw this precious one deeply into You, so that he or she may see and hear and know the truth of Your heart. And Lord, may this truth bring deep rest and strength and all that this person needs right now, whatever circumstances he or she is facing. I ask these things in Your precious Name.
JESUS.

"JESUS WEPT"

It was September 11, 2001—and Jesus wept.

An airplane hit a building. Another airplane hit another building. A third did the same, and a fourth crashed into an open field.

Lives were taken—so many lives. And others were left behind to somehow piece life together without those who were taken—

husbands and fathers
    wives and mothers
        daughters and sons.

Mrs. O'Neil; Baby Jillian; Grandpa Johnny; best friend, Steve . . .

It was the most awful of days: A day of heartache and grief, pain and loss. So much pain, so much loss. It was September 11, 2001—and Jesus wept. . . .

Let my eyes overflow with tears night and day without ceasing; for . . . my people has suffered a grievous wound.

It wasn't the first time, however. Those weren't the first tears the Son of the living God shed in the face of human suffering. That wasn't the first day His divine heart was pierced and splintered by death and dying, brokenness and pain.

"Lazarus is dead."

Two thousand years ago, as a flesh-and-blood Man with a flesh-and-blood heart and flesh-and-blood feelings, Jesus stood facing a friend's grave. It was another day that Jesus' heart broke.

A woman named Mary lay in the dirt at His feet, wailing in grief. Lazarus was her brother. He was Jesus' friend. And he'd been snatched from this world much too early, torn from their lives before his time. Now the Son of God stood staring at his grave, and He wept. Lazarus was dead, and Jesus wept.

The event is recorded in chapter 11 of the Gospel of John, and the moment is so significant that it's given its own verse: 35. It is the shortest verse in the entire Bible, and its two words are whispered so simply, so humbly—so shockingly human, so emotionally bare.

Could the writer really mean the Son of the living God? "Jesus *wept?*"

Before Abraham was born, I am.

After all, Jesus is King of kings and Lord of lords. He is

the Lion of Judah

the Rock of Ages

the same yesterday, today, and forever.

As a Man who walked the earth two thousand years ago, He was Immanuel—"God with Us"—the living embodiment of the living God, the human revelation of I Am Who I Am.

Once Jesus was asked to "show us the Father." We can only imagine the set in His jaw and the smile on His face as

He turned and joyously proclaimed, "Anyone who has seen me has seen the Father" (John 14:9). In other words, *"You're looking at Him, guys. As I am, so is God!"* Glory to His blessed Name!

But surely such stature, such distinction, would suggest someone who is stoic, immovable, divinely composed. A Man who is God would surely walk high above such earthly realities as pain and loss, serenely beyond such human "untogetherness" as heartache and grief. Surely Jesus stood unaffected by the blows of life that assault you and me.

At least that is how we often picture Him—detached and ethereal, unfeeling in His divine supremacy. We often speak and write of Him that way. That is how we approach Him in prayer. In many of our church traditions, we present Him that way, and that is how we tend to portray Him in art and film.

We've all seen the Renaissance paintings and stained-glass images of the elegant Man standing high above the common folk groveling at His feet. His arms are extended wide; His face is long and expressionless; His demeanor is pious and aloof. His eyes are passively fixed toward heaven. We expect Him to speak in Shakespearean baritone, using lofty words like "thee," "thou," and "thine."

But the portrait painted of Jesus in the Gospels of Matthew, Mark, Luke, and John is a far cry from such religious fiction. In the truth of His divine and living Word, in the Holy Spirit–inspired canon of holy Scripture, we meet a Man who is quite shockingly the opposite. We meet a Man who is breathtakingly "real"—more real, more down to earth, more dirt-under-the-fingernails authentic than any man who has ever been.

[He] made Himself nothing.

We see Jesus in the streets day after day, offering people His kingdom in exchange for their pain. We see Jesus feeding the hungry masses, reaching His carpenter-callused hands into the filth of a leper's sores, washing people's feet, starving in the wilderness, lifting cripples out of the sand, pulling prostitutes into His embrace. We see dirt and fatigue, struggle and striving. We see a Man on a mission like no man has ever been on a mission before or since.

As long as it is day, we must do
the work of him who sent me.

What is aloof about being born in a barn? What is supreme about sleeping in open fields? What is detached and serene about falling on your face and crying over lost people?

O Jerusalem . . . how often I have longed to gather your children together, as a hen gathers her chicks under her wings.

What is so lofty about having your blood drip in the sand as people spit in your face?

JESUS.

Yes, in Scripture we see Jesus in His reality—His passion and persistence, His drive and desire. In His Word we see Him in His truth—the King of kings dressed in blood, sweat, and tears, day after day pouring Himself out, hanging from wood, pouring Himself out even more. We see Him for who He really is—Jesus.

Praise His precious name!

And standing before His beloved friend's grave that day, face to face with loss and death, we see Him weep. "Jesus wept," the Scripture says. We see Him weep . . . *Jesus weeps.*

I don't know, but I've got to think that a really good

friend was something rare for Jesus two thousand years ago. After all, He was the living God in human manifestation. Can you imagine how alone that must have left Him?

Who can know the mind of God?

Who could possibly understand a Man who singularly walked in the fullness of God's understanding? Who could possibly relate to a Man with such vastness of perspective, with such infinite depths of divine contemplation? Talk about being on a different page!

And His life was so public and controversial. Day after day He was followed, picked apart, pursued for so many of the wrong reasons.

It is only by . . . the prince of demons, that this fellow drives out demons. (Matthew 12:24)

We want to see a miraculous sign from you. (Matthew 12:38)

He is worthy of death. (Matthew 26:66)

Can you imagine, day after day—*after day after day*—living like that?

Oh, how He must have hungered in His human heart for the love and companionship of a flesh-and-blood friend! How he must have longed for that someone we all long for—that someone with whom He could share a meal at the end of a hard day. That someone with whom He could confide all His aloneness. That someone who wouldn't judge Him or need something from Him—who wouldn't try to fix everything or tell Him what was best for Him. That someone who would just

be there for Him
    take the time to care
        care enough to listen.

I wasn't there two thousand years ago, so I can't say for sure; but Jesus retreated so often to Lazarus's home, I think it's a good bet that Lazarus was that someone. It's a good bet that Lazarus was a flesh-and-blood friend Jesus could feel at rest with. That confidant Jesus could lean on. That buddy Jesus could just hang out with and chuckle with over silly things, and maybe—for just ten minutes—not have to be so very important.

But as wonderful and blessed as close companionship

is, it isn't free. Not for anyone—not even the Son of God. No, there's a price to be paid for so precious a friendship. Depth of love, height of relationship: These are life's greatest treasures; and accordingly, they are life's greatest costs.

So the day came when Lazarus simply was no more. The day came when Jesus' friend was ripped from His life. Jesus' companion was torn from His heart, removed from His experience. There were no words between them; no tender good-byes. There were no tearful hugs, no whispers, "I love you." Lazarus was just . . . gone. Yes, death touched Jesus' life, just as it touches yours and mine.

"Where have you laid him?"

And so He wept. One hundred percent Man, one hundred percent God—He stood before His friend's grave and wept.

JESUS.

Different theories tack deep spiritual meaning and profundity to His brokenness that day—theories that rob Jesus of His humanness and heart and, at the same time, condemn us for ours. I heard a preacher once say that Jesus wept because the people had no faith that He could raise Lazarus from the dead.

But two thousand years ago Jesus *was* human. Jesus *did* have a heart. And to the family and friends of Lazarus who saw Him with their own eyes that day, there was no question about that. To the people who stood next to Jesus at that grave, who witnessed His tears spilling in the sand, there was no deep spiritual meaning attached to those tears; there was no hidden significance.

As they looked on—some standing as close to Him as these words are to you—the source of His grief was abundantly clear. "See how he loved him!" they whispered to each other (John 11:36).

And it's true: Jesus did love Lazarus. Oh, how Jesus loved Lazarus! In the perfection of His heart—a heart that beat completely free of all the

> reserve and caution
> > self-protection and fear
> > > questions and complications

that we who are far from perfect so commonly bring to the table of love—Jesus loved Lazarus. He loved him so, so much.

How wide and long and high and deep is the love of Christ, . . . this love that surpasses knowledge.

And so He wept. By that width, that length, that depth, that unknowable measure of His perfect love—oh, how Jesus wept.

How His face must have collapsed into the calluses of His carpenter's hands, the mass of His shoulders shaking under the weight of His fully human grief. How His tears must have spilled, perhaps His frame folding to its knees in the sand beneath His bronzed and weary feet. Lazarus was dead, and Jesus wept.

Sometimes when "things happen," we mortal folk feel very alone in our struggles and grief. We feel alienated from the people around us—maybe even abandoned. We feel distant from God—perhaps even abandoned by Him.

Sometimes we even feel ashamed. We feel like total failures as people, getting nowhere as we wrestle to cope and overcome. We feel like failures as children of God too; because as much as we know the scripture, "Be filled with the Spirit. . . . always giving thanks to God the Father for everything" (Ephesians 5:18–20), we think, *I just can't give thanks for this situation.*

So we kick ourselves: *Grow up!* Our friends encourage us: "You've got to move on." Good and godly counsel seems to taunt us: "Count it all joy" (James 1:2 NKJV).

Then there's Jesus. Reaching His Spirit-hand to lift the mortal countenance, speaking through the healing salve of His healing Word, He gently whispers into your heart and mine:

"I know your tears, My child. I cried them Myself, and I know. You are so precious to Me. I love you . . . and I know."

JESUS.

"BEFORE ABRAHAM WAS BORN, I AM"

I don't know about you, but it is far beyond me to even begin to picture a man who is God . . . who just happens to be a man . . . who is also God . . . but God as a man who is equally and simultaneously God . . .

*And they will call him Immanuel
—which means, "God with us."*

What does that look like—"God with us"? Can you imagine a man who walks through life with the same mind as any other man, but who thinks with the mind of God? A man who wakes every morning with the same heart and emotions as any other man, but whose heart also beats with the feelings and emotions of the Almighty? This man's heart explodes and leaps with the same hope that gave birth to everything that was created through His omnipotent hand—everything from the stars in the midnight sky to the oceans that crash upon distant shores; from the splitting of the Red Sea to the splitting of His own flesh.

JESUS.

What does a man who is God act like? I mean, in a private moment when no one is watching—one of those moments that never got recorded in Matthew, Mark, Luke, or John?

Jesus did many other things as well. If every one of them were written down, . . . even the whole world would not have room for the books that would be written.

As silly as it may sound, what does that man eat for dinner? What does He think while He eats it? After all, His were the Spirit-hands that created it. He devised it and sculpted it. He knows every molecule, every neutron and electron. He scripted its every life function. He birthed it in His divine imagination; and thousands of years earlier, He foresaw the day He would be sitting there eating it.

Through him all things were made; without him nothing was made that has been made.

Or does He just eat? Does He not think about those things—only about the human hunger in His human belly? Like any other human, does He simply think about what would satisfy that hunger most, and eat?

What does He think is fun? What kind of jokes does He tell? How does He react when someone says something foul? What does He do to "get away from it all"—or does He even *have* that desire to get away from it all?

And when He cries as He did before Lazarus's grave, surrounded by Lazarus's grieving family and friends—why does He cry harder than everyone else put together?

He groaned in the spirit.

What does He know in the midst of those tears that is so far beyond what anyone else knows? What is it that causes Him to groan deep within His spirit—and weep?

JESUS.

As the heavens are higher than the earth,
so are my ways higher than your ways
and my thoughts than your thoughts.

Jesus was God, pure and simple. The heart that shattered within Him that day at His friend's grave, that Lazarus day, was not only the heart of a Man weeping for the loss of someone close and dearly loved—as if that weren't painful enough. *It was the heart of the living God.*

Who among us can possibly claim understanding of such a reality? Who among us can wrap comprehension around

the vastness
the breadth
the dimension

of what it means: the heart of God in the heart of a man? Who among us can begin to fathom even a corner of the compound layers and infinite depths of His divine perspective?

And who among us could possibly bear the heartache that most surely flows from that perspective? It is heartache that you and I will never begin to know; and standing by that graveside, unbeknownst to anyone around Him, Jesus was swallowed up in that heartache like you and I don't ever want to know.

For the wages of sin is death.

We tend to accept death as—well, as a part of life. We're ripped apart when it imposes its inescapable reality upon the circle of those we know and love. But what can we do?

"You've got to move on."

"These things happen."

"That's life."

But death is not life, nor even a part of life. Death is the exact opposite of life. It is the absence of life, the lack of life—the removal of what was created to live and enjoy life.

It is the fallout, the price, the "wages" that you and I and all of creation have paid and continue to pay for doing things our own way and turning our backs on His way.

And here's the huge truth that cries out to be understood, to be contemplated, to be dwelled upon and grieved over just as Jesus grieved over it on that long-ago Lazarus day, just as He grieves over it this day and every day: *Death was never something God intended for any of us to taste or endure.*

There He is, the Son of the living God standing before the grave of Lazarus, cloaked in the indignity of human flesh; and "having been" from before the beginning, He alone understands. He alone knows the fullness of the tragedy and the horror of the horror: *None of it ever had to be.*

His human eyes stare at the stone that hides His human friend's remains, but His divine eyes see far beyond that stone into the horror hole of what that stone represents. The horror hole of everything His Father never wanted to happen. The horror hole of sin's abominable decree.

In the wide-angle scope of His divinity, He sees it all:

the crushing of life
   the tearing of spirit from flesh
      the wretched finality of corruption and decay.

He sees it all—and He alone understands: *None of it ever had to be!*

Oh, the wound that it tears in His holy heart! He stands weeping—His human feet soiled with the dirt of a human burial ground, His human heart crushed by the death of a man He dearly loves. He stands weeping—His divine feet fixed across the expanse of divine understanding, His divine heart crushed by centuries upon centuries of death upon death of oh, so many men, women, and children He dearly loves.

JESUS.

Surrounded by Lazarus's family and friends, His human ears are swallowed in the agony of human mourning. Their weeping and wailing swirls around Him from every side; their voluminous cry is an unholy deep closing its mouth over the respiration of His holy soul.

Oh, how it all caves in on His heart—how it beats and batters and rips at His being. He's the Son of the living God; and in solitary awareness, everything inside of Him revolts and repulses, cries and collapses: "*No, no! None of this was ever meant to be!*"

Yes, "the wages of sin is death" (Romans 6:23). The literal enormity of that truth is a cold, merciless spearhead thrust through His divine flank, as it would be so literally thrust on Calvary in weeks to come. It jabs and jabs at His heart, carrying

every drop of blood ever spilled
   every disease and calamity
      every death rattle and final breath

and every tear that you and I ever shed or ever will shed in the wake of these horrors.

JESUS.

And as His heart claws for air through the tidal wave of all that pain and understanding, again, having been there "from the beginning," His divine memory is freshly awakened. His mind courses back, back, back . . . to "that" day.

That first day.

That *very* first day.

It was centuries of earth-years earlier, but to Jesus it's as if it were yesterday. It's a day that haunts Him—the day that caused Him to rise from His throne and plunge Himself into humanity. It's the day that drives this Lazarus day, that drives His every day. And deep within, He remembers it all . . .

A man and a woman stand beneath a tree. It's a fruit tree—an extraordinary fruit tree. It's a tree their Father has placed in the middle of their garden and given a name:

"The Knowledge of Good and Evil."

It's the one tree that the man and the woman have been told to stay away from—"You must not touch it." Its fruit is the only fruit they have been cautioned not to eat—"or you will die" (Genesis 3:3).

But—isn't it just the hallmark of human nature?—it is the one tree the man and woman can't seem to stay away from. Its fruit is the only fruit that makes them wonder, *What would it taste like?*

And so a choice is made. Innocence is sold. Immortality and perfection and goodness are tossed away for the baubles of appetite and curiosity.

She took some and ate it.

Oh, heartbreak of heartbreaks! It is tragedy eternal. If only they'd trusted Him. If only they'd obeyed!

But they did not. And now they stand, the man and the woman, naked and silent. For the first time, suddenly, a strange new reality is upon them—she is not smiling, and neither is he.

Then the eyes of both of them were opened.

33

The man looks away from the woman, though he doesn't know why. The woman slides behind the tree, though she doesn't understand it. And as the fruit stains their lips, so also it stains Creation. As its juice drips from their fingertips, so also it seeps into the tapestry-weave of eternity itself.

The supple breeze that always was suddenly cuts like a cold wind. The clouds that used to skate gaily across the sky's expanse suddenly gather, thick gray overtaking blue. And the birds—where are the birds? The garden always danced to a symphony of birds, but suddenly there is silence. As far as the ear can hear, only silence.

Cursed is the ground.

And right on cue, extending an upturned claw through the center of creation's rent, sin greedily demands its initial due. An animal is slaughtered for its skin. That which was intended to warm a beast now hides the man, now masks the woman. First blood is spilled. Death has begun. The wheel cogs of human suffering creak into motion and commence their unforgiving grind.

Yes, standing by His friend's grave—that grave that need never have been—Jesus remembers that ancient day all too well. He remembers the tears He shed and the tears His Father shed. He remembers even more the tears the man and woman shed.

He remembers their shame, their hiding. Oh, how it broke His heart to see them hiding! He only loved them; why would they hide? He remembers

> their fear and confusion
>> their doubt and difficulty
>>> their toil and strain

in the days that followed. He remembers their hunger, their arguments, all the times they got hurt and fell sick—struggles that would become their daily lot because of their choice that day.

Now Cain said to his brother Abel,
"Let's go out to the field."

He remembers when their elder son, Cain, drew a club against their younger, Abel. He remembers the ebb of the boy's blood as his frame folded and dropped in an open field. The innocence in the boy's eyes as they looked up and silently pleaded, *Why?* The whisper of the boy's last breath. The silencing of the boy's last hope.

He remembers the primal wail that rose from the lungs of the man not an hour later. The agonized shriek that exploded from the woman. The way she ran and threw herself on her son. The way the man cradled his limp body in his arms. He remembers the tears they cried that night—inconsolable tears, night after night.

Yes, He's the Son of the living God, and He remembers—He remembers it all. Now dressed in the costume of physical reality, staring into the black gluttony of His friend's grave, the memory lashes His heart as it has for centuries—a razor-edged refrain slicing afresh the timeless and ancient wound: "The wages of sin is death."

None of this was ever meant to be.

And so His holy heart breaks. Oh, how His heart breaks! Under a crush unimaginable, the human anguish descends on Him from one side, while the divine anguish buries Him from the other.

Into a million pieces
　　in a million places
　　　　in a divine depth

that you and I will never begin to know, His heart breaks. It breaks, and it breaks, and it breaks.

JESUS.

We struggle to imagine it: a perfect heart within a perfect God within a perfect man breaking—in any circumstance. We mistakenly interpret that word *perfect* to mean invulnerable. We think of a heart that's so "together," it's beyond being bruised.

But isn't it really quite the opposite? A heart never moved is called hard and dysfunctional. A man who can't cry is to be pitied above all.

But a soft, sensitive, supple heart—one that is open and feels deeply—*that's* a good heart, a perfect heart. It's a heart that loves in all of love's fullness and in spite of love's costs.

In a matter of weeks, Jesus, who now stands before His friend's grave, will willingly pay those costs. He will restrain all the power of the kingdom of heaven and allow foreign brutes to drive nails through His hands and feet. He'll hang from a piece of wood. His blood will drip into the soil. He'll cry, "It is finished," and then give up His spirit.

How much softer can a heart possibly get? How much more broken over love that's been lost? How much more desperate for love to be gained?

"Greater love has no one than this, that he lay down his life . . ." (John 15:13). Greater love. Greater heart. How much breathtakingly greater can they possibly be?

JESUS.

"WHY, O LORD?"

"If it hurts Him so much, why does He allow terrible things to happen?"

It's the age-old question: If God is who He says He is, then why all the pain in life, why all the horror? Why in heaven and earth doesn't He do something? Why doesn't He intervene?

How long, O LORD?
Will you hide yourself forever?

It's a question that was asked the whole world over on the morning of September 11. It's a question that's been asked a million times by millions of people caught in the grip of millions of private and personal "September 11s."

It's a question that was asked two thousand years ago, on that first-century September 11, as Jesus faced Lazarus's grave.

Swirling all around Him as He stood there weeping was a froth of arrogant whispers: "Could not he who opened the eyes of the blind man have kept this man from dying?" (John 11:37).

Oh, the aloneness of Jesus! They wouldn't even allow Him to grieve.

He had given everything that they might have life and life abundantly (see John 10:10). In the coming days, He would give even more that they might have life and life *eternally*. But such treasures, it seems, are paltry to men and women. On this Lazarus day—a day like every day—these treasures were met with abundant complaints and grumblings. They were met with gossip and opinions eternally.

"Why this?"

"How come that?"

"You're not who You say You are. I can tell by what's happening to *me!*"

Man judging God: It is the most widespread of crimes, the very oldest of professions. Man assuming that his wisdom and understanding is superior to that which hurled the sun into the afternoon sky: What a horror! What a slap in His face!

JESUS.

In the pages of Scripture, the answer to every question, every accusation, lies free for the seeking, obvious and true:

For all have sinned and fall short of the glory of God. (Romans 3:23)

The wages of sin is death. (Romans 6:23)

For the creation was subjected to frustration . . . [and] bondage to decay. (Romans 8:20–21)

In the way of righteousness is life, and in its pathway there is no death. (Proverbs 12:28 NKJV)

Then there is the most answering scripture of all—words from the lips of Jesus Himself as He spilled His heart on the pavement of Jerusalem's temple courts for everyone to see: "How often I have longed to gather your children together, as a hen gathers her chicks under her wings, but you were not willing. Look,"—open your eyes and see!—

"your house is left to you desolate" (Matthew 23:37–38).

It's true: The "desolations" that you and I suffer in this life are not the product of an aloof and uncaring God. How uncaring can He be—to step out from heavenly glory to be born in a barn, to work with His hands, to sleep in the fields, to suffer the mockery of common men, to be hung like a rag on a tree?

For God so loved the world.

Are such choices born out of apathy? No, they're born out of care—care beyond what any of us could imagine *care* to be. They're born out of passion and hope and desire. They're born out of longing—His longing. His longing for you. His longing for me.

In the book of Revelation the apostle John records a heavenly vision that captures this passionate longing, this unimaginable care. It is a startling image, a shocking revelation that very well could be the most revealing in all of Revelation: Standing in the center of the throne of heaven at the right hand of the Father is a lamb, "looking as if it had been slain" (Revelation 5:6).

JESUS.

It is God's devotion in a single image. It is His response to mankind's rebellion and sin; the passionate urgency with which He reaches and woos; the unyielding commitment He extends—even as man continues to scoff and laugh in His torn and battered face.

You are worthy . . . because you were slain, and with your blood you purchased men for God.

No, the problem is not Jesus. The hole in Creation through which evil oozes, gurgles, and putrefies everything in its wicked and vicious path is not a hole torn by an angry and distant God. It's a hole ripped open by us: "But you were not willing." In the grip of our sin nature, it's a hole torn by you and me.

Inch by inch
   generation by generation
      sin by sin

and rebellion by rebellion—wider and wider the hole is torn by a billion yous and a billion mes across the expanse of time and humanity. Like a silent crawl of consuming lava, like an avalanche roar, it grows and it grows, as does the danger it presents. Ravenous and insatiable, it swallows and destroys everything in its random and reckless path.

To you I call, O LORD my Rock; . . .
Hear my cry for mercy.

And may we make no mistake; may there be no illusion. Sin takes no prisoners. Horror plays no favorites. It doesn't pick and choose who will be its next victim. It doesn't decide who deserves all and who deserves none. It just flows and flows. It reeks and reeks. It feeds with gluttonous frenzy on anything close and everything near—you, me, the good people next door—vomiting disease, desolation, and tragedy all the more.

Cancer strikes; drunkenness flows. Dad has heart disease; Mom doesn't hear like she used to. Two cars collide; a family writhes in divorce. A gunshot splits a big-city night; a child is stolen on a small-town day. An airplane hits a building; Jesus weeps before His friend's grave.

Come quickly to me, O God.
You are my help and my deliverer.

All of it is the fallout, the by-product, the putrid refuse of sin. It infiltrates, cripples, and rots the very Creation of which you and I are a part. It can never be said too often or strongly enough: Not a pin-drop of it did He ever want to be!

And yes, He could easily intervene. In the past He has intervened; and as His Word guarantees, He'll intervene in the future even more. The day will surely come when all the laughter that's done in the dark will be paraded openly in the light. All bets will be called in. Right *will* prevail.

He will turn back upon them their own iniquity. . . .
The Lord our God will wipe them out.

Truth be told, He intervenes in the here and now too. But his intervention seldom looks like we want it to look; and in our world of

shouts and screams
bells and whistles
racing from this to that

it comes in a whisper that cries to be heard. But He intervenes nonetheless—24/7, He intervenes.

There isn't one of us in the midst of our choices who doesn't hear His still, small, intervening voice in the private place of our conscience. *"No,"* He whispers. *"That's not the way you should go. That way will surely lead to your harm. That path will devastate your family."*

There isn't one of us in the midst of our choices who doesn't walk by His still, small, intervening voice sitting, leather-bound, on our coffee tables and bookshelves. *"Sin leads to death; don't take the risk. I have plans for your future; walk in My ways. Remember mercy, holiness, self-control. Come to Me and I will give you rest for your soul."*

A man sits on the couch, beer in hand, and clicks on the TV. A preacher is there. "Friend," the preacher pleads, "Jesus died for your sins and offers you the free gift of eternal life." The man hears the words—words as intervening as words can be. He swigs his beer. He makes a choice. He flips the channel to football . . .

A woman follows her friends into a dark, loud place. The music pounds, the laughter echoes. Smells of perfume and sweat, whiskey and leather collide. A man she doesn't know touches her as if she did. The Lord whispers, *"This guy doesn't care. He'll only hurt you."* The woman hears the plea; for a moment, perhaps, she even listens. She makes a choice. She touches the man in return.

A husband and father packs a suitcase. His pastor said no, his friends and family said no; and through every one of them, the Lord begged him, *"No!"* But the car is running, and a young woman waits. He pulls the ring from his finger. He makes a choice. He closes the bag and heads for the door . . .

People making day-to-day choices in their day-to-day freedom to make their own choices. And oh, what a terrible price is paid for that privilege—

what tragedy
what pain and loss
what brokenness.

It is a price born by the chooser and, willfully or otherwise, imposed on everyone in the chooser's path. It's imposed on every life and heart, every child and grownup, every stranger and stranger's family who just happens to be in the vicinity when the horrific choice is made.

*Now choose life, so that you
and your children may live.*

I picture a man in a cheap motel room. An angry man. A man far from the country of his birth. Day after day, night after night, for many days and many nights, he has been sitting in the company of cigarettes and coffee, take-out pizza, and inexpensive beer. He has a plan. A well-thought-out plan. A plan that will cost lives—many lives, he hopes.

A cell phone, a rented car, maps, cash: It's all ready. It is September 10, 2001. And unbeknownst to the nation that has opened its arms to him, come sunrise he will park his rented car in an airport parking lot and execute his plan.

How many times did this angry man sit at coffee-shop counters, and through the smiles and gentle conversation of people he'd been taught to hate, hear the living God cry, *"No! It's all lies. These people are good, and everything you've learned is lies!"* How many times in how many of those faces did he picture men and women lying beneath the rubble of his freedom to make choices— even as the living God continued to plead from deep within, *"What you're planning to do is wrong!"*

How many times did he pass a little boy or girl, their mother holding their small hands, and think of all the little boys, all the little girls, who would suffer the fallout of his decision—perhaps even his own little boy, his own little girl? How many times did his own basic sensibilities revolt against what he'd set his mind to pursue? How many times did the living God explode through that window of sensitivity and plead and plead, *"No, no, no!"*

And it's so far outside our capacity to accept, I know—but how many times and in how many ways did the living God try to reach in to save his eternal soul?

It is not the will of your Father who is in heaven that one . . . should perish.

I picture this same angry man weeks earlier, driving through town on a Sunday morning. Perhaps he stops at a red light, and his attention is suddenly arrested by music and singing cascading through open windows from a church on the corner. It is unlike the rote, religious chanting he is accustomed to. It is warm and exciting, joyous and alive.

With every note and chorus, the living God pleads at the door of the angry man's heart. With tears unceasing—tears for the angry man and tears for the lives he plans to destroy—the living God begs and begs, *"Come! I'll give you rest for your soul."*

But the angry man's answer is no. He makes a choice. The light turns green, and he slides his foot from the brake to the gas pedal. He drives on, maybe in fear, maybe in confusion. Maybe the anger and lies are just

so entrenched
    so enthroned
        so rampant

—so "Legion"—that he just drives on.

Or maybe the angry man hesitates. Maybe something deep inside him cries out for freedom from all the lies—for any excuse to escape and run from them. Maybe the vise grip strangling his heart has hurt so much for so long that his heart longs to breathe, longs to know truth and joy.

And maybe on the wings of that music coming from the church, a whisper of God's cry to him slips between the cracks of his yearning. For a moment he thinks about turning his wheel and driving his rented car into that church parking lot. And in that moment, all the angels in heaven get their dancing shoes ready in anticipation of another life saved—*of thousands of lives saved.*

But then maybe there is another man in the car behind him who isn't so angry but forever in a hurry—a self-important hurry. Maybe he grows impatient with the angry man in front of him; and in his same freedom to make choices, he blasts his horn, shattering the softness that was beginning to take hold in the angry man's heart.

Maybe, God forbid, the impatient man is about to turn into the church parking lot himself. *O Lord, let it not be so!* Maybe in his hurry to get to God, he makes a liar out of God in the mind of the angry man.

And maybe the angry man becomes even angrier. Maybe that impatient blast kicks and twists the life-giving words that God has been speaking and, in the skilled hands of hell's manipulation, actually affirms the lies. Maybe it leaves the angry man even more convinced that his cause is just, that his evil perversion of right is right indeed.

But have no fear—the living God is not a God who gives up on anyone, especially with so much at stake. So He continues to reach and reach, pursuing ever more, inviting and intervening, never tiring, never ceasing, pleading and pleading: *"Jesus, Jesus. Come to Jesus!"*

Where can I go from your Spirit?
Where can I flee from your presence?

Maybe the angry man stabs at the radio as he drives his rented car, and there is that music again—the exalted worship of a Christian broadcast. Leaping through the car speakers with outstretched arms, the living God trumpets His glory in invitation: *"I've set before you the path of life. Choose Jesus!"*

Later the man clicks on the TV in his cheap motel room and hits upon a preacher's passion. Again the Spirit swarms his heart: *"Jesus, Jesus! 'I am' Jesus!"*

Each day before September 11, he drives past cross after cross on hilltop and steeple; and like the blood of Jesus that flowed two thousand years before on Golgotha, the testimony spills and splashes against the walls of his willingness. Its impassioned shout reverberates in his soul and spirit: *"Eternal life! Come to Jesus!"*

How many men and women did the living God send along the angry man's path—in a post-office line, on a bus ride to Florida, at a donut-shop counter? How many of His children did the living God nudge and prompt, beg and lead, *"Go talk to that guy about My Son. Go talk to him about Jesus!"*

He is the living God, and His beckoning is constant, desperate, through every means imaginable—desperate, astoundingly so, for even the angry man's life. Desperate— oh, how desperately desperate—for the lives of the many the man hopes to destroy.

Seek me and live.

Untiring, unyielding, passion unceasing, the very voice that spoke heaven and earth into existence cries out to the very last seconds: *"Steer away! Choose Jesus! Steer a—"*

But the answer is no. Like the cold steel of a Roman spear, an airplane thrusts itself through the living God's heart. Like the cruel mass of a Roman crossbeam, tons of concrete crumble upon His back. Like His blood that flowed till there was no more, the voluminous cries of the dying and wounded, the broken and shattered, the wives and husbands, parents and children pour forth into the dust and soot-filled morning air.

And so He weeps. *"My babies, My babies! Look what they did to My babies!"*

He weeps

and He weeps

and He weeps.

JESUS.

⸻

This is the verdict"—He phrases the words with human lips on a distant Jerusalem night, two thousand years ago—"light has come into the world. . . ." His voice breaks; His gaze turns away. Divine foresight swells from within His eyes and spills down His very human cheek-bones, staining the weave of His most blessed beard.

"But men loved darkness instead" (John 3:19).

JESUS.

CHAPTER FOUR

"MY EYES FAIL, LOOKING FOR MY GOD"

"Still, God should do something. I mean, *really* do something. *Anything!* He's God, isn't He?"

It's the very same cry that began the last chapter, just turned up a notch—a notch toward angry. Angry at God. We don't like to talk about it too much, and few of us who've been there will easily admit to it. But we do get angry.

Thankfully, it's not so rare a sound to His everlasting ears; and my goodness, it's often so entirely understandable!

On September 11, for example, people were struck from out of nowhere, crushed and torn by a never-imagined barrage of agony, confusion, and loss. There were wives whose husbands lay beneath that rubble. Children who went to

school that morning, never to see their mommies again.
People died. Lives were shattered, families destroyed. Years
have passed, and to this day people cry.

*I am worn out from groaning; all night long I flood
my bed with weeping and drench my couch with tears.*

Angry at God? Oh, how understandable! He alone had
the power to do something. "But He did *nothing!*"

The Sunday after, men in suits took to podiums and
stood before television cameras, trying from the pages of
Scripture to answer that cry. Right or wrong, valid or not,
compassionate or cold, we heard every explanation under
the sun and then some:

"God is judging America."

"We're seeing page twenty of Revelation."

"This is the beginning of revival."

"It's all in His master plan."

But the truth of the matter is, "Who has known the
mind of the Lord?" (Romans 11:34). "How unsearchable
are . . . His ways" (Romans 11:33 NKJV). As Job worded it
after forty-one chapters of trying to figure it all out:
"Surely I spoke of things I did not understand, things too

wonderful for me to know" (Job 42:3).

And completely aside from September 11, born in the anguish of countless lives caught in innumerable personal and private tragedies and losses, the angry fists are shaken in His face every day. Thousands upon millions of fists are shaken. Maybe you've shaken your fist—or I've raised mine.

But if there's one scripture that no biased fool would even attempt to debate, it's this one: "There is nothing new under the sun" (Ecclesiastes 1:9). In the Daddyhood of the living God, the tear-stained ire of His children is as ancient as days . . .

It is three thousand years ago, and the living God has just liberated an entire nation from generations of Egyptian slavery and hell. For hundreds of years His children cried and shook their fists; and now, rising from His throne as *El Olam*, *El Elyon*—the Everlasting, the Most High God— He has answered their cry.

I have heard them crying out . . . So I have come down to rescue them.

He's reached into Creation with the tip of His pinky and flipped the immutable laws of nature up one side and down the other on their behalf. He's imparted blood-judgment. He's intervened and intervened and oh, so miraculously intervened.

Pharaoh summoned Moses. . . . "Take your flocks and herds, as you have said, and go."

Then He decides to intervene even more. He slides up His almighty sleeves, bares His almighty arms; and, as if out of the pages of a novel too incredible to believe, He splits open the Red Sea and then slams it shut, consuming their enemies in front of their eyes, never to be seen again, never to torment them again. Oh, glory to the living God!

But He has barely resettled in His heavenly seat, hardly had a chance to enjoy the celebration and laughter of His babies at His feet, when—*can it really be true?* The same fists, the same anger—*all shaking in His face all over again!*

Then the whole congregation of the children of Israel complained.

May there be no indictment, though. The people had run into difficult times; and difficult times, let alone serious tragedies, have a way of getting to the best of us. They strip us of everything we know and turn our foundations to quicksand. They swipe all recollection of our Daddy's goodness.

We Christians do our best to smile and talk about things like faith, God's purpose, forgiveness. "Count it all joy," we say through strained lips. Other folks do their best to smile, too, and find some way—somehow—to be strong and "keep on movin' on." But late at night, in the aloneness of our rooms when no one is watching, we cry. We shake our wounded fists, because that's all we can really do—"I just don't understand, Daddy!"—and we cry.

What have I done to You, O watcher of men?
Why have You set me as Your target?

Yes, sometimes at the end of all there is to know, all we really know is that it hurts.

"I want it to stop, Daddy. Won't you please just make it go away?"

JESUS.

It is two thousand years ago, and in the tiny village of Bethany, a woman named Mary sits quietly by a bedside and watches her brother, Lazarus, die. She has already called every doctor and prayed every prayer. She's done all that she could do and then some. Now her heart begs for mercy; her hope says, "No more." She cradles her brother's hands, measures his every breath.

Now a certain man was sick, Lazarus of Bethany.

Her gaze turns toward the open window. She reflects the great times she and Lazarus used to have together— so many great times. She reminisces about his smile, his grace. With a chuckle she remembers the tough-guy look he would always give when any boy came by to visit her.

She remembers the way she and her brother would sit together—oh, for hours they would sit together!— watching the sun melt behind the surrounding hills, enjoying the evening air. They would laugh and laugh and tease with each other. Then they would grow quiet and share their dreams . . .

She remembers the day they both met those dreams, all in one man named Jesus. He was so common, so ordinary—a Galilean to boot. He was a working man just like her brother, just like Lazarus. But He did such magnificent things!

She remembers the first time they saw Him perform a miracle. A beggar from their village was filthy with the disease of leprosy. Head to toe, he was nothing but infection and rot. But Jesus touched him. He got right down in the dirt with this ghastly leper and actually touched him!

She was horrified. *How could anyone touch him?* Lazarus was disgusted and furious. Touching someone who was "unclean" according to the Law of Moses, the Law that Lazarus loved and esteemed—what a grotesque violation!

He grabbed his sister's hand to pull her away. But then they saw the tears in the unclean man's eyes. They saw his shame, his fear, his rejection. Suddenly he wasn't an "unclean man" to them anymore; he was just a man. He was a man the same way Lazarus was a man. And oh, what a terrible disease for any man to have to endure!

And Jesus—it was as if He knew all that. As if He understood. It was as if He could actually feel the man's pain—yes, that was it!—*as if it were His own.*

And oh, how Jesus cried that day. He actually took that man in His arms—took in his filth, his smell, his disease, his everything, and held it all against His own chest. And He cried. The sight turned her stomach and took her breath away all at the same time.

What kind of a man would do such a thing? What kind of person could this Jesus be?

Then she saw it happen. It happened so fast that she still wonders if it really happened. Jesus lifted the man's face, whispered something into his ear, and—how to even begin to comprehend or convey what she saw next?

All the sores and infection
    all the deformed and twisted flesh
        all the skin that looked like scales

—they all went away. As if they were never there in the first place. *They all just went away!*

I am willing. . . . Be clean!

The people around the man shrieked. Never had anything like this been seen or imagined. Lazarus—oh, sweet brother, Lazarus—fell to his knees, gasping to breathe. And the man—he screamed and screamed. Shouts of joy! He kept looking at his hands and grabbing his face, and he just screamed. Like a child's skin, his face was. Like silken cream!

"I'm clean!" he kept shouting. "I'm clean! I'm clean!" In a billionth of a second of time, in the blink of an eye, he was *completely clean!*

JESUS.

Lazarus sat and stared into nothingness the rest of the day. He wouldn't eat; he wouldn't do anything. He just sat on that little bench outside the door and stared. Then deep in the night—she'll never forget it—she heard him whisper, through the window above her room, over and over to absolutely nobody, "What kind of man is this? What kind of man could this Jesus be?"

To think they would all become friends! No, not just friends; dear, best of friends. She remembers the first time Jesus came for supper. She was so nervous, she didn't say a single word the entire evening. Oh, how embarrassing it was—and leave it to Lazarus to never let her live it down.

But who could blame her? Here He was, Messiah Himself, sitting at their table like anyone else would sit at their table. She could barely look Him in the eye. She could barely breathe!

Not Lazarus, though. Lazarus had a million questions, and Jesus was going to answer every one of them. Sitting by her brother's bed, she dabs his brow with a cold towel and smiles at the memory. Poor Jesus that night—Lazarus hardly gave Him five seconds to eat His food.

Then there was their sister, Martha, just running around like a crazy person. "Is everything okay, Lord? Can I get You this? Can I get You that? Did You like the lamb? Oh, no, You couldn't have liked the lamb! I'm so sorry about the lamb . . ." It's a miracle that they ever saw Jesus again.

But they did see Him again—and again and again. He would sit at their table many times after that first night; He would sleep on their floor. And they would become friends—good friends. Especially He and Lazarus—oh, they were such good friends!

Jesus loved Martha and her sister and Lazarus.

She remembers them working in the field together, swimming in the stream, and laughing while sitting at the table. She remembers them rising before dawn every morning to tiptoe outside. Once she creaked open the door to spy on them, and what she saw took her breath away. These two men she loved most in all the world were on their knees together, wrapped in blankets against the cold, singing praises to Jehovah God.

Yes, they were the best of friends, Lazarus and Jesus.

That's what makes this all the more crazy to her. That's why it makes no sense that she is at his bedside, watching her brother die. She's struggled and struggled and done her best to listen to all the arguments and explanations:

"Jesus is busy."

"Jesus is too important."

"It's not in His Father's plan."

Even Lazarus had told her, in a lucid moment, that she shouldn't feel the way she feels. But still it seems to her so absolutely crazy.

So the sisters sent word to Jesus,
"Lord, the one you love is sick."

She'd watched Him heal complete strangers. There was that leper, for one. Why would He heal the leper but not her brother who loved Him so much? Where is the sense in that?

But that's not the offense. That's not what *really* stings. What really stings is that *He didn't even bother to come.*

He stayed two more days in the place where He was.

He knows. She knows that He knows. But He's not here. Her brother, His so-called "dear friend," is dying, and He hasn't even bothered to come.

So many times Jesus had looked them all in the eye and said, "I'll never forsake you." She believed Him—they all believed Him—and here He didn't even bother to come. So many times He'd taken her face in His hands and smiled, "I love you with an everlasting love." She'd trusted those words. She'd trusted that smile. She'd given Him her heart as Lord and friend—and here He didn't even bother to come!

Can you imagine Mary's woundedness, her sense of betrayal? She'd chosen "the better way," as Jesus worded it. She didn't just *believe*, like so many others—*she loved Him*, like so very few.

This Mary, . . . was the same one who poured perfume on the Lord and wiped his feet with her hair.

And so her brother dies, and four days too late word

arrives: "Jesus is on His way." Oh, what insult is heaped upon Mary's injury! *Now* He comes? The pain and confusion must surely have wrestled against His reality within her heart. *Now* He comes, when "the one He loves" is already in the grave?

In much of Christian tradition, Mary tends to be idealized; and the thought of her being angry at Jesus may be something of a shock to religious imagination. But truth be told, Mary was very much human. She was very much the same as you and I, subject to the same doubts and confusion we have; the same grappling when His words don't seem to line up with our events; the same wondering sometimes and battling other times.

And even if she did have an extraordinary understanding of Jesus or a greater-than-our-own amount of faith, is there even one among us who has *never* questioned? Is there one who has *never once* struggled in hurt and tearing of heart when the Lord's silent inaction seems so at odds with the truth of His Person and the promise of His Word?

Listen to the cry of Israel's beloved King David in words he wrote a thousand years before Mary was born, three thousand years before you and I came on the scene:

"How long, O LORD? Will you hide yourself forever?" (Psalm 89:46). "Why, O LORD, do you stand far off?" (Psalm 10:1). Yes, even the best of us has writhed and squirmed in the grip of that confusion; and King David notwithstanding, the best of us may well have been Mary.

In Jesus' absence her brother has died. In Jesus' silence she feels her trust impaled, her love for Him slapped in its face. Is it any wonder that she doesn't run to meet Him along with her sister, Martha? Is it any wonder that she stays right where she is, surrounded by friends? *Real friends*—the sentiment must surely have sprouted from the torment in her heart—*friends who truly care.*

[Martha] went out to meet him, but Mary stayed at home.

But then Martha returns with a message for her sister: "The Teacher is here, and He's asking for you." Oh, that bitter crossroads at which each of us has stood! Do we bow to what we see and cling to what we feel, or do we blindly—yes, blindly—entrust ourselves to Jesus?

What does Mary do? She bolts from her home and rushes to Jesus. Was it

a spike of hopeful desperation?

an act of superworldly trust and faith?

an explosion of fury born in grief?

No one can say for sure why she ran. But finally she's face to face with Him; and under the concrete tonnage and twisted steel of agony and exhaustion, she falls at His feet and vomits her confusion in understandable complaint: "Lord, if You had been here, my brother would not have died" (John 11:32).

How many times has the same cry erupted from our own lips? How many times have you and I thrown ourselves prostrate, when not one of "the rules" made even the slightest sense; and, stripped of all religious posture, wailed from a depth of soul we never knew existed: "Why didn't You do something? *Why*?"

Again, hear the same cry from the very same struggles of King David—a man we esteem, a man God Himself called "a man after my own heart" (Acts 13:22)—"My God, my God, why have you forsaken me?" (Psalm 22:1).

Can't you hear his frustration and heartache? And so far beyond that, his sense of abandonment and angst? Yes, when life and its circumstances of tragedy and disease, brokenness and loss collapse upon our lives, and you and I and Mary feel that exact same way, we're not such spiritual failures. *We share in the company of God's most chosen king!*

Hear, O LORD, and answer me, . . . Guard my life, for I am devoted to you.

And so on that Lazarus day two thousand years ago,

faithless and hurting
    naked of heart
        in honest desperation

and utterly void of religious poise, Mary collapses into the sand before Jesus and cries unashamedly.

"Lord, if you had been here, my brother would not have died."

Injured and bruised, confused and exhausted, she drowns His feet in the tears of her private "twin tower" that's crumbling around her—*And it is then that Jesus weeps.*

He stands in that moment nothing less than the living God, wrapped in the flesh of a common man. He's the Creator of the universe, the Everlasting to Everlasting, cloaked and disguised in human simplicity. He's all Majesty, Power, Glory, and Honor; and as He looks upon Mary, stripped of everything by grief, writhing in the pit of her confusion about Him and how this could happen and why it would happen; as He looks at her family and friends broken alongside of her, He weeps.

There is no teaching that comes from His divine lips. There is no parable, no rebuking of Mary or anyone else for unbelief. There is no disapproval of Mary's impassioned expression, no religious posturing or pious restraint.

There is only compassion, understanding, heartbreak, and personal pain.

Broken by Mary's brokenness
   torn by her torn-ness
      pained over her family's pain

crushed by that which crushes you and me—*as if it were His own*—Jesus weeps. He weeps, and He weeps, and He weeps.
JESUS.

And with every human tear that spills and splatters at His human feet, His every divine yearning cries out that you and I would understand:

"This is who 'I am,' My child. You are what's in My heart, and this is who 'I am.'

"I weep for what causes you to weep. I mourn for what causes you to mourn. The things that break you break Me— and oh, so much more.

"I love you, My child. I live and die with you—I lived and died for you—and I love you. Yes, you, *My child—it's* you. *I love* you. *"*

JESUS.

CHAPTER FIVE

"NOT A SPARROW FALLS . . ."

That Lazarus day two thousand years ago wasn't the only day that Jesus wept. Neither was September 11. There were other days too—oh, so many other days.

How precious also are Your thoughts to me, O God! . . . If I should count them, they would be more in number than the sand.

On September 11 you and I, the entire country, most of the world—we were halted, torn, and consumed by the horror of that morning, and rightfully so. We stood before our television sets, and we cried. Some stood in Manhattan, Pennsylvania, Boston, and Washington, D.C., waiting for word about someone they loved—and, heartbreak of heartbreaks, they cried so much more.

It was a day of such unimaginable horror! Those of us who weren't directly affected will never begin to know the extent. At the same time, the terror assaulted all of our lives on one level or another with the fullness of everything horror can be.

But as terrible as that day was, in the eyes of heaven and within the divine heart behind them, what qualifies as horror is not defined by the magnitude of its drama or the exceptional nature of its degree. In the eyes of the living God,

any tragedy
any loss
any and all brokenness

looks like horror; and it's all just plain horror, no more or less horrific than all horrors.

Precious in the sight of the LORD
is the death of his saints.

Little Johnny got hit by a car on September 10. The world didn't know anything about it—but Jesus did. Jesus knew all about it, and He wept.

Suzy lost her mommy on September 9. It didn't make any of our headlines, but in heaven—in the vastness of His oh, so vast heart—Suzy's loss was front-page news.

Ruth's only daughter died in the womb. That was back in August. Ruth had been trying and trying, and praying and praying; and then she got pregnant, and she and her husband were so excited—and then . . .

Phil's only brother fell to heart disease. Believe it or not, it was Christmas Day. Funny, but that was always Phil's favorite, Christmas Day.

Then there were January 6 and February 5—and oh, the horrors that took place on March 16! There was April 3 and May 12 and June 25, and that endless stream of tragedies that splashed scarlet across the living God's heart all through last summer.

There was the seventeen-year-old girl who was assaulted in July, while on summer vacation. She was walking along the beach, enjoying her young life, thinking about her young future, basking in the leisure of the soft, summer days. Then "he" came like a predator, like a filthy monster—and oh, how Jesus wept. Oh, the horror it was in His heart!

I have indeed seen the misery of my people.

Can't you see the pool of holy tears that flood the legs of His holy throne? Not on one day or two days, or because so many lives were affected here, or someone was so particularly cruel there. But every day, because of every horror—day after day after day after day. Los Angeles, California. South Bend, Indiana. Toronto, Canada. Brisbane, Australia. Green Bay, Wisconsin. Johannesburg, South Africa. Day after day after day . . .

"My babies, My babies! Look what they did to My babies!"

JESUS.

You see, to you and me it's, well, again, "part of life." We live in a broken world full of broken people who do broken things and struggle through broken circumstances. We're just so accustomed to brokenness.

We were born into brokenness, and we walk every day surrounded by brokenness. We even turn on our televisions and entertain ourselves with brokenness—crime scenes, emergency rooms, soap operas where every husband cheats on his wife and every wife manipulates and connives against her husband.

We walk into movie theaters and pay money to watch brokenness—spectacular explosions, parents who are buffoons, drunken cops, murder, mockery of virtue. We buy video games for our children that make a sport of brokenness—"Blood Games," "The Evil Within," "Mission: Annihilate."

Our hit songs are all about brokenness—"My baby left me, and I've got no reason to live." "Without you I'm nothing." "Alone again." One of our most beloved and celebrated music genres is even called "the blues." It's such wonderful music; but step back and really give it serious thought: Why would anyone want to sing about feeling blue, feeling down? Even more, why would anyone want to hear about it—about being abandoned, rejected, hopeless, alone?

Son of man, take up a lament.

It's truer than true: Our familiarity with brokenness has, at its least, jaded us to its bleakness; and, at its most heartbreaking—I can't believe I'm actually writing the words—become something strangely "good."

Yes, you and I have become very accustomed to brokenness. And there's no condemnation there; it's a necessary accustomedness that allows us to keep going and make something of this life in spite of its brokenness. It's even a hallmark of bravery—to keep marching through the brokenness.

But then there's the living God and His living understanding. He knows what He truly created life to be, and oh, how horribly off the mark it has become.

I know the thoughts that I think toward you.

In His eyes, "twin towers" didn't fall only on September 11. That wasn't the only day that sin imposed itself on His kingdom's order and His babies' innocence. It wasn't the only day that life was stolen—life in the physical and life in the soul; life in the fullness of every glory, goodness, health, and wholeness of life He ever intended to be.

Just ask any father who's sat by a hospital bed and watched his child's monitor flat line. Ask any wife whose husband has said, "I'm no longer interested," and walked out the door. Ask any eight-year-old boy whose home is in an alley, whose days are spent begging for bread. Ask any eighty-year-old man who's been tossed to an institution and left by his children for dead.

Yes, "twin towers" fall every day. In the whisper of private lives all around us, they fall. As much as September 11 was "yesterday," for someone close to me as I write this and close to you as you read this, it's September 11 today. And there,

> in the midst of it all
>> so singularly aware of the horror of it all
>>> gripped in the agony of every loss of it all

the living God weeps. He weeps, and He weeps, and He weeps.

My eyes fail from weeping . . . because my people are destroyed.

JESUS.

A twelve-year-old boy comes home from school one day and finds his house strangely empty. The morning dishes remain in the sink, and the beds have yet to be made.

There's no note from anyone anywhere.

Quietly he goes about his after-school business—the refrigerator, the TV, maybe some homework once he clears the kitchen table. He drops his favorite CD in his Discman and goes about his usual routine. But for reasons he can't explain, he has a "funny" sense deep inside. It's a kind of tiny, twelve-year-old panic. *Something is very different.* It nags him. *The house is empty, and something has changed.*

Come four o'clock the boy hears his father's Ford Explorer pull into the driveway, and the panic rises. *What's Dad doing home so early?* The front door opens, and, strangely, his parents are together. *Why is Mom so dressed up in the middle of the day?*

"Come sit down," she says, forcing a smile and patting the sofa next to her. *This isn't good,* his instincts scream. *Run away!*

"Your father and I have been to see a lawyer," she calmly continues. "Some things are going to change . . ."

With every word that flies from his mother's mouth, a 767 slams into the boy and destroys his everything. His life, his world—the Pentagon of his home and security—

all destroyed. Hidden beneath his twelve-year-old cool and composure, a veritable fireball rips through the twin towers of his heart and reduces them to rubble.

And when the fallout of ash and debris settles, the scene is nothing short of carnage. Hope and trust, peace and confidence, sureness and love and a child's self-understanding—they all lie broken and lifeless, scorched beyond recognition, scattered, crushed, and in pieces.

What remains are the concrete ruins and twisted steel of anger and fear, doubt and despair. What remains are some new things that were never God's plan for his young life, things he'll "just have to get used to"—half of a dad, half of a mom, being tossed from one to the other. Abandonment, rejection, loneliness . . .

It's a scene played out in countless living rooms across America and around the world on any given day. Unseen by you and me, as commonplace as any scene could be, it makes no headline. It causes none of us who aren't involved to even skip a beat.

And yes, the boy will survive—millions of them do. But the living God weeps. He feels the magnitude of the horror. He absorbs the boy's brokenness and pain. He weeps.

CHAPTER FIVE

My heart is poured out on the ground . . . because children and infants faint in the streets of the city.

It's also true that He will redeem. In the mass of His mercy that so dwarfs any human horror, His Plan B for the boy is already in motion. In divine foresight, long before the day of destruction, He began the business of resurrection and redemption.

But it was never His intent that the boy go through such agony. It was never His plan for the boy's family to melt and crumble. It was never His will for the boy to suffer like that. And all too aware, He invests His compassion in the boy's every teardrop. He submits His own heart to be crucified on the boy's same tree.

"My babies, My babies! Look what they did to My babies . . ."

JESUS.

It's the middle of the night, Big City Hospital, Anytown, Anywhere. A family stands huddled around a much-too-young woman snagged in the grip of a terrible disease.

It has been a long, hard-fought battle, and they've stood with her every step of the way. They were there when the surgeons took her first breast; they were there when she sacrificed the other. They were there to drive her home from chemo, and they were there when she picked out her first wig.

It has felt like years—not just for her, but for all of them. So many doctors. So many prayers. Now, having exhausted every resource and option, exhausted in every imaginable way, all they can do is tell her they love her—to be by her side on this most final of days.

Oh, what a tragedy that Creation is so infested with sin's vile infiltration! It was never God's plan that this woman's body would be plundered as a member of that Creation. Such disease was never His perfect intent.

Sin entered the world . . . and death through sin.

So in the fullness of His Spirit, right alongside her family, He weeps. He is more her Father than her dad, more her Husband than her mate. He loves her more than all of them together, and His omniscient anguish is so far beyond all of their tears. And so He weeps, *"My babies, My babies . . ."* The living God weeps.

How we cry out to Him in the grip of our tragedies! We beg Him for comfort, for healing, for freedom from our pain. But who comforts *Him*? What shoulder bears the weight of His infinite tears? What escape is there for His heart, so immeasurably impaled by such immeasurable pain?

Surely He has borne our griefs
And carried our sorrows.

"How precious to me are your thoughts, O God! How vast is the sum of them!" (Psalm 139:17). What price He must pay for such vastness of care. What price He must pay for such vastness of heart!

Yes, the living God weeps. He weeps, and He weeps, and He weeps.

JESUS.

84

"BY HIS WOUNDS WE ARE HEALED"

Then comes the day that Jesus lies still on a frame of raw wood, and all the 767s of life that have thrust their horror upon you and me and everyone around us are hammered through His hands and driven through His feet. Like a lamb led to the slaughter, the Son of the living God hangs from a cross beneath the beauty of His heavens and surrenders Himself to horrors never imagined on earth.

His appearance was so disfigured beyond that of any man . . . his form marred beyond human likeness.

It is far beyond mortal comprehension that the Creator of the universe would choose to join you and me in human suffering—and then suffer beyond what you and I ever need endure. It is a mind-spinning reality that He who alone need never taste torment would choose a feast of torment.

But on Golgotha that's exactly what Jesus does. He is Alpha-Omega—He Who Always Was, Is, and Always Will Be—and He bows Himself to the consequences of human sin. He is Adonai—Lord Master—and He submits Himself to the cruel hand of corruptibility. He is King of kings and Lord of lords—God in the Flesh—and He baptizes His own being in the cesspool of human adulteries.

He poured out his life unto death. . . . The LORD has laid on him the iniquity of us all.

It is shocking, the reality of Jesus that crucifixion day. The most cold-hearted and conscience-seared among us couldn't handle knowing even half of it.

Perhaps that's why the Lord allows it to remain largely hidden beneath the veil of poeticized wording, glamorized art, and religious presentations. Perhaps that's why He allows our general familiarity with the story to so rob us of any cutting-edge appreciation for what really happened. Perhaps even in that robbing, undetected and unrealized, lies a testimony to the quantum measure and intricate involvement of His boundless mercy: The truth is so beyond horrible, He spares us true understanding!

*I am poured out like water, and all
my bones are out of joint.*

But may none of us be cheated by a lukewarm or casual consideration. That day on Golgotha two thousand years ago was a September 11 day unlike any day before or after.

"The wages of sin is death" (Romans 6:23), and "the LORD has laid on him the iniquity of us all" (Isaiah 53:6). These may be very familiar words to some of us, and they may sound philosophical and theological to others; but if, for just a moment, we were to step back and stare down the black hole of exactly what they mean . . .

*He was pierced . . . he was crushed . . . it was
the LORD's will to crush him.*

Sin. Iniquity. Death. And not just *death* death, if you know what I mean; but the death that takes place in life too—death in broken families and broken hearts

> broken bodies and broken trust

>> broken circumstances and shattered hopes.

Yes, death takes many forms and enjoys a multitude of layers and degrees.

And in the middle of it all, at the end of it all, the fallout and by-product of it all, the bottom line and culmination of it all: *pain*. Oh, such pain! Phenomenal, incomprehensible, immeasurable across generation upon generation and upon nation after nation. Pain, pain, and more pain—"and the Lord has laid on Him the iniquity *of us all*."

JESUS.

Can any one of us even begin to imagine? *All* of the pain, *all* of the brokenness, *all* of the horror, *all* of the loss, *all* of your grief, and *all* of mine—all of it that all of us put together have ever known and ever will know, and then some—borne on Golgotha by the Son of God.

Every killing and every rape. Every war and every genocide. Every act of slavery, imprisonment, and greed. Every wife who's ever been slapped, every child who's been molested. Every pencil that's been stolen, every automobile that ever slammed into a tree. Every father left abandoned, every mother cheated on. Every cancer, every disease, every Third World starvation. Every shame, every betrayal, every fear and frustration . . .

He was cut off from the land of the living; for the transgression of my people he was stricken.

It goes on and on—human history from day one to beyond, written in sin and painted in all the agony that is its result. And every inch of it—

every cry ever uttered

every tear ever wept

every drop of blood ever spilled—

descends and caves in on Him, all on that Golgotha day. It swallows Him from below. It chews on His soul. It beats and batters and grinds His Person, all in one incomprehensible September 11 moment of one incomprehensible Golgotha day.

My God, my God, why have you forsaken me?

That's the "debt" that Jesus paid. That's the price, the "wage" He relinquished for our sin. That's the "race"

He bled to complete.

He abandoned Himself to hell in its ultimate degree. He invited it to do with Him whatever it would please. "The punishment that brought us peace was upon him, and by his wounds we are healed" (Isaiah 53:5).

JESUS.

A long, long time ago a man and a woman ate fruit from a tree they knew they shouldn't touch. Their nakedness turned to shame, and all of Creation writhed in its very first agony. Centuries later, the Son of the living God hangs exposed from a tree He need never have known. Children spit on His nakedness. Their laughter paints Him with shame as He writhes in the vice grip of Creation's same agony.

Behold! The Lamb of God who takes away the sin of the world!

Not so long ago—perhaps today, as I write this and you read it—a father and a mother make a decision to end their son's life. A surgeon's tool intrudes into the woman's womb. *Mommy, Daddy, why have you forsaken me?* The killing begins, and the son is no more.

Two thousand years earlier, another Father makes a decision to end His Son's life. He turns His back—oh, what it costs Him to turn His back!—and all of hell intrudes. "My God, My God, why have You forsaken Me?" (Psalm 22:1 NKJV). The killing begins, and the Son is no more.

The LORD makes his life a guilt offering.

It is September 11, 2001. A fireman rushes into a tower built of concrete and steel to save people he doesn't know. The tower will fall; and, heroism beyond heroism, heartbreak beyond heartbreak, the fireman will become one of those he sought to save.

It is Golgotha, somewhere around A.D. 30. The Son of the living God rushes into a tower built of sin and all of hell's horror to save people *He longs to know.* The tower will fall; and, heroism beyond heroism, heartbreak beyond heartbreak, the Son of the living God will fling His arms wide and welcome its collapse upon Himself, all for those He will now have a chance to know.

What shall I say? "Father, save me from this hour"? No, it was for this very reason I came to this hour.

There is pain out there in this thing we call the world—very real, very crushing, not-to-be-thought-of-lightly pain. It is my hope that you have somehow been spared the worst of it. At the same time, I'm very aware that you may know it heart-breakingly well. But in all sensitivity, just for a moment, please allow me to suggest and allow yourself to consider: There is no pain that can even come close to the pain of Jesus.

Take all of your pain and all the pain of everyone around you, multiply it a billion times a billion times a billion—and you've got that day. You've got Golgotha. You've got, "For God so loved the world that He gave His only begotten Son" (John 3:16 NKJV). Yes, you've got Jesus.

Roaring lions . . .

    open their mouths wide against me.

I am poured out like water,

    and all my bones are out of joint.

My heart has turned to wax;

    it has melted away within me.

My strength is dried up like a potsherd,

    and my tongue sticks to the roof of my mouth;

you lay me in the dust of death. . . .

they have pierced my hands and my feet.

(Psalm 22:13–16)

JESUS.

We ask the question, "Why do bad things happen to good people?" And there in the middle of that question hangs the only One who is truly good. There in the middle of it hangs Jesus.

We ask, "If God is so good, why is there so much pain in the world?" And there in the middle of that cry, taking on Himself every inch and every moment of all the pain in all the world, hangs Jesus.

We ask, "Why doesn't God do something?" And with every drop of His precious Son's blood, He looks up from the pool of His tears—tears upon tears—and answers us all: "I did do something. See? There hangs My Jesus."

And when Jesus had cried out again in a loud voice, he gave up his spirit.

JESUS.

"BUT REJOICING COMES IN THE MORNING!"

At the end of all the tears and weeping, at the end of all the pain and trauma, the moment would come when Lazarus would incredibly rise from the decay of his departure. The moment would come when the breath of life would descend from heaven and explode into his lungs, and every tissue and organ, every cell and molecule, would be instantaneously reconstructed, reawakened, and shaken alive!

"Lazarus, come forth!"

At the end of all the tears and weeping, at the end of all His incomprehensible pain and trauma, the moment would come when Jesus Himself would also rise. The moment would come when the Spirit of the living God—

His Spirit
   the Father's Spirit
    the Holy Spirit

—would rush His dormant remains and trumpet, "Live!" into the limpness of His limbs, the silence of His heartbeat, the blackness in His eyes. "Live, live, *live*!" Glory to Jesus!

He has risen, just as he said.

It was His plan for Lazarus all along, when all anyone could see that Lazarus day was tragedy and loss. It was His plan for Himself, if I may, when all anyone could see that Golgotha day was even greater tragedy and greater loss.

Two thousand years later, it is His hope for you and me that we would come to Him with all of our tragedy and loss. That we would fall before Him as Mary did, and cast it all at His more-than-capable feet. That we would give Him the chance to reach His miracle-working hand into every corner of it and do what He so loves to do—what only He can do: resurrect and redeem!

Weeping may remain for a night,
but rejoicing comes in the morning.

As Mary sobs before Jesus, caught like all of us in the blinding twister of personal crisis, how could she possibly foresee the resurrection He has waiting up His glorious sleeve?

"Where have you laid him?" Jesus calmly speaks. Then with steely resolve: "Take away the stone" (John 11:34, 39).

Shock spreads across Mary's face. Shock drops across every face of every person standing there with her. The words blow their minds sky-high. What a grisly suggestion! What a grotesque absurdity!

As it is, no one dares make a move. "But Lord," they object, "he has been in there for four days." Translation: "The situation is beyond redeeming; it's outside the realm of any hope. There is only blackness and void, and there is no good You can possibly do."

To human eyes there never is. But standing there that day, Jesus alone comprehends the infinite scope and rock-solid sureness of what only He can entirely know: "With God all things are possible" (Matthew 19:26).

"Take away the stone!"

And suddenly there He is, staring into the black hole of His friend's grave, eye to eye with the foulness of this thing called death—this thing that was never supposed to be. Yes, far beyond the still body of Lazarus, there lies "the wages of sin" in all its totality of ugliness, licking its filthy chops and grinning up at Him like some vicious beast. There it lounges, a vile glutton, so grossly pleased with itself for all the torment and suffering it's ever had the pleasure of vomiting onto you, onto me. Onto Him.

Not many days earlier, Jesus had stood in the center of a Jerusalem crowd and magnificently proclaimed His purpose: "I have come to give you life and life abundantly!" Now He stands face to face with everything that opposes His purpose—everything that strives to steal life—every decrepit enemy that seeks to crush and kill and rob us of all His intended "abundantly."

The thief comes only to steal and kill and destroy.

Within the lifelessness of that grave is everything that Jesus hates, everything He's come to reverse and set us free from. Within the decay of that grave is everything of horror and of hell to its worst, destructive degree. Within the pain of that grave is every private and public tragedy that ever was or ever will be.

He loathes what He sees in the darkness of that grave; He despises all that it represents. He sees every moment of its deadly decree, from the day Abel's blood was spilled at the hand of Cain to the September 11 morning in Manhattan and Pennsylvania and Washington D.C.

Within that grave is the day Suzy lost her mom; that horrendous rape; the cancer that couldn't be stopped. Within that grave is little Johnny and the car accident that took his life; Phil's brother, and the heart disease that just wouldn't let go. Within that grave is Ruth, and her baby that was never born; that twelve-year-old boy, and his family that was torn apart.

You who've lost sons and daughters, husbands and wives, mothers and fathers, dear friends, and so much more—ever-so-tragically so much more—please, please know:

Everyone who has ever suffered through any level of loss or disease, betrayal or family tear, painful crisis or broken circumstance, please, please know:

He's the Son of the living God, and He not only stands before Lazarus's grave but before the grave of all losses—your losses and mine. In its blackness He sees them all. In its silence He hears every tear that you and I have and will ever shed in the night.

JESUS.

Now He stands, a mountain of a man, the undefeatable enemy of everything that would dare to be our enemy, icily staring down the throat of that grave. He is

the Creator of the universe

the Everlasting to Everlasting

the Power that laughs in the face of all power,

unconquerable beyond eternity; and He prepares to teach the grave a lesson in who's Boss with three simple words: "Lazarus, come forth!" (John 11:43 NKJV).

Can you imagine the eruption of righteous thunder in His voice? Those three words trumpet the essence of His being, the purpose of His nature, the delight of His Person, the declaration of His desire: *"Let there be an end to death and dying! Let there be an end to sin's rule! Let there come forth joy and hope among the living, and eternal life among the dead! Come forth! Come forth! Let everything that is Lazarus in every one of My babies' lives come forth!"*

JESUS, JESUS, JESUS!

And oh, what a celebration erupts in the heavenlies! Lazarus stumbles out of the blackness and into the light, and all of eternity explodes in joy and excitement beyond comprehension. Legions of angels and heavenly beings dance and whirl: "Lazarus lives! Lazarus lives! He who was dead once again lives!" Oh, glory to the Name of Jesus!

I am the resurrection and the life.
He who believes in me will live.

It would be only a few weeks later that Jesus Himself would follow suit. On the heel of Golgotha's horror, His dried blood still staining Golgotha's sand, those who loved Him still dressed in black, the stone that sealed His own tomb would be rolled away. He Himself would triumph unimaginably over the finality of the grave. He Himself would rise in that Lazarus joy—that joy that is His promise to you and me. That joy that comes "in the morning."

After three days . . .

Yes, three short days, and He who tasted death beyond

death would send it cowering and running for its very life (pun fully intended). He is the Son of the living God, the Lion of Judah; and, make no mistake, He laughs majestically in death's powerless face.

He hoists Himself alive and rises to His feet. He steps out of the grave's blackness and bursts into the brilliance of His own creation's sun. He slings back His head and shakes His mane free. He thrusts His hands skyward and laughs and laughs, then lets out a conqueror's roar!

*Go quickly and tell his disciples:
"He has risen from the dead."*

Yet again the heavenly multitudes explode in joy. Oh, my goodness, can any one of us even begin to imagine the joy? "He lives! He lives!" They celebrate and celebrate. "He is King of kings, triumphant in glory, forevermore unto all eternity! He is Jesus, *and He lives!*"

And for you and me these two thousand years later, the proof is again made. Oh so thunderously, the hope is declared. The unalterable promise of God is emblazoned upon every moment of your heartbreak and mine, upon every tear ever born in every loss: *Rejoicing comes in the morning!*

For whatever reason unknown to me but very known to Him, those words may be very hard for you to trust and believe right now. "The morning" may seem light-years away—if it's ever going to come at all. But you know what the breathtaking thing is? He understands that. After all,

He's walked through loss
    He's tasted hard times
        He's experienced pain

He knows all too well how crippling they can be.

But for the record—I just have to say it, because it's truer than true; and by His Holy Spirit, may it be made alive in every one of our souls—the living God longs to reach into whatever pain or loss is in your life and do what only He can do: resurrect and redeem. It is His hope, and it is well within His power. It is His deepest desire, whatever your situation may be.

Come to me . . . for I am gentle and humble in heart; and you will find rest for your souls.

And rejoicing will come. Many mornings may pass before "that morning," but His promise is true. Rejoicing *will* come. No mountain of pain is bigger than He is, no sea of loss more vast. No grave is deeper than His passion to reach, no death stronger than the tenderness in His hands. No ruin is more enveloping than the brawn of His embrace, as He bends to lift you free from whatever darkness surrounds you.

And He loves you. He loves you so, so much.

JESUS.

I will never leave you nor forsake you.

If you could see His face with your physical eyes, oh, the smile you would see—because He loves you. If you could hear His whisper with your physical ears, oh, the warmth, the genuineness you would hear—because He loves you. If you could feel His physical arms around your shoulders, pulling you gently to His holy chest—my goodness! The understanding, the sureness . . .

"I love you, My child," He whispers. *"It's true. And I have such plans for you to live. I know—there's been*

so much that doesn't make sense
so much to endure
so much to carry.

I know those things. I know. But you must trust Me, My child. It's all you can do. Just take away the stone—all the anger, all the fear (yes, I told you, I know), and come forth and live.

"Oh, how I love you, My child. Come forth and live.

"Yes, take My Spirit-hand. Come to Me—and live. Live, live, live!"

JESUS.

"LET US FIX OUR EYES ON JESUS"

It was with these words that we began so many pages ago, and I can't think of more significant words for us to close with these many pages later.

Everything that's been written in this book has been written with you in mind, recognizing that you may be going through a difficult time in one way or another. It may be a time of deep and serious loss; and if that's the case, may I pull over to just say that I'm so, so sorry. There's no way I can even begin to understand everything that you're feeling. Such things are so intensely personal. And not knowing you or the nature of your loss . . . I'm just so, so sorry.

Maybe you're fighting your way through a serious illness

and trying to hold your family together at the same time. Maybe you've been betrayed, and your heart is broken in pieces. Maybe terrible things happened when you were a kid, and now those things haunt you. Maybe your dad and mom just split up, and you're reeling from the explosion. Maybe you *are* that dad or mom, and wherever the fault may lie, you're reeling too.

Tough times come from so many angles and in so many ways. And as common to the human experience as any of them may seem—oh, how none is to be taken lightly; how all are to be handled with greatness of care and compassion!

I will never forget an afternoon long ago, when I was asked to speak to a group of people who had been through some very hard times. Having never been through those particular struggles myself, I felt grossly unqualified, and all I could think to do was pray and beg the Lord to somehow touch their lives.

I remember praying a very specific prayer in that regard, and the Lord's response just blew me away. I prayed, "How can I minister to these folks, Lord? I don't know them." Just as quickly as those words leaked from my lips, it was as if the Lord replied in the privacy of my heart, *"You don't have to know them, Bruce. I know them. I know*

> *every struggle and every heartache*
> > *every hope and every circumstance*
> > > *every brokenness and every tear.*

You don't have to know them, Bruce—I know them."
JESUS.

And even the very hairs of your head are all numbered.

I realized then that my job that day was not so much to resolve the people's crises, but rather, simply, to show them Jesus—to present Him in such a way that they would somehow understand Him a little bit more and know His heart for them right in the middle of it all.

Well, here I am years later, and—isn't it just like the Lord?—my job is exactly the same; and I can only pray that somehow through these pages you've caught a fresh glimpse of Jesus, a glimpse of His heart—His heart for you right in the middle of whatever you're going through.

No matter how hard it may be to believe right now, He's the living God, and He has plans for your future. And it's not a matter of, "Where's your faith? Buck up and dive in!" Oh, how cruel and heartless some counsel can be!

I know the plans I have for you.

It's more a matter of just falling into His arms—kind of like Mary did that day in Bethany so long ago. It's a matter of casting all of yourself onto Him, understanding that His tears fall right alongside yours; and in that kinship of heartache, saying, "Jesus, I don't get it, and it just hurts so much . . . but I love You. I need You so much, and I love You."

"And I love you, My child," He responds. I don't care whether you're full of excitement over Jesus or full of anger toward Him; His response is exactly the same. He stands with His Spirit-arms stretched toward you, His eyes glistening with care for you, and a smile on His face from here to heaven—*"Yes, I love you . . ."*

JESUS.

I am the bread of life.

And He continues:

"In this world, My child, there will be trouble. I know that all too well, because in this world I had trouble. But there is great cause to take heart, My child. I have overcome the world, and hand-in-hand I will lead you through it. I promise you, I will lead you through it.

"Peace will come, My child—peace beyond understanding. Rest will come—rest for your soul. And I know it's hard for you to believe right now, but joy will come too. There is joy that comes in the morning.

"So come to Me, My child. Yes, just come to Me and continue to come to Me. That's all you need to do.

"I'm gentle, My child. I'm humble in My heart—and I love you. Oh, how I love you. I love you, I love you, I love you . . ."

JESUS.

I have loved you with an everlasting love.

Yes, at the end of the day, when all is said and done, no matter where any one of us is in our lives, we just need Jesus. Whether we fight against it

 or celebrate it

  or refuse it completely—

oh, how we need Jesus. So may I ask, do you know Him in your heart as your Lord and Savior? I ask because that's where it all begins. Without access to your life, He has no opportunity to love you the way He so desires—no way to reach in and mend, heal and redeem.

If you confess with your mouth, "Jesus is Lord," and believe in your heart that God raised him from the dead, you will be saved.

Pray along with me, won't you? Invite Jesus into your heart: *Jesus, I need You. Come into my life; come into my heart. Free me from my sins; heal my heart and mind. I need You, Jesus. I need You. Amen and amen.*

That's so wonderful! Now go out and celebrate your new life with Jesus. Grab a Bible and go to the book of Romans and the Gospel of John, so you can learn more about Him and what it means to have Him in your life. Go to the book of Psalms, and you'll see your very same struggles played out on the pages. Find yourself a good Bible-teaching church, jump in, and simply enjoy growing in Jesus. Praise His blessed Name!

There will be more rejoicing in heaven over one sinner who repents . . .

But you know, chances are good that if you've taken the time to read this book, you know Him in your heart already. And that's great. What a glorious thing! Now draw close to Him, brother. Draw close to Him, sister. Cut away everything that gets in the way. Cast every concern, trouble, and heartache at His feet and pursue Him with all of your heart—just as He so pursues you with all of His.

He loves you. He loves you so, so much. And the day will come when you will look Him in the eye, and all the things that don't make sense will simply disappear in His overwhelming and undeniable goodness. He'll wipe away every tear that day. He'll take you by the hand and replace all of your mourning with a dance of extraordinary joy.

And God will wipe away every tear from their eyes;
there shall be no more death, nor sorrow, nor crying.

Live for that day. "Fix your eyes on Jesus"—just as
His eyes are oh, so fixed on you. Lean into His heart,
and rest your everything in the embrace of His eternal
whisper:

"I love you, I love you, I love you . . ."

And surely I am with you always,
to the very end of the age.

JESUS!

SCRIPTURE REFERENCE NOTES

INTRODUCTION: "LET US FIX OUR EYES ON JESUS" (HEBREWS 12:2)

Consider him: Hebrews 12:3
You will . . . find me: Jeremiah 29:13
Streams of tears flow: Lamentations 3:48
He was pierced: Isaiah 53:5

CHAPTER 1: "JESUS WEPT" (JOHN 11:35)

Let my eyes overflow: Jeremiah 14:17
Lazarus is dead: John 11:14
Before Abraham was born: John 8:58
[He] made himself nothing: Philippians 2:7
As long as it is day: John 9:4
O Jerusalem: Matthew 23:37
Who can know the mind of God: 1 Corinthians 2:16, adapted
Where have you laid him: John 11:34
How wide and long and high: Ephesians 3:18–19

SCRIPTURE REFERENCE NOTES FOR PAGES 25–53

CHAPTER 2: "BEFORE ABRAHAM WAS BORN, I AM" (JOHN 8:58)

And they will call him Immanuel: Matthew 1:23

Jesus did many other things as well: John 21:25

Through him all things were made: John 1:3

He groaned in the spirit: John 11:33 NKJV

As the heavens are higher than the earth: Isaiah 55:9

For the wages of sin is death: Romans 6:23

She took some and ate it: Genesis 3:6

Then the eyes of both of them were opened: Genesis 3:7

Cursed is the ground: Genesis 3:17

Now Cain said to his brother Abel: Genesis 4:8

CHAPTER 3: "WHY, O LORD?" (PSALM 10:1)

How long, O LORD: Psalm 89:46

For God so loved the world: John 3:16

You are worthy: Revelation 5:9

To you I call, O LORD, my rock: Psalm 28:1–2

Come quickly to me, O God: Psalm 70:5

He will turn back upon them: Psalm 94:23 AMP

Now choose life: Deuteronomy 30:19

It is not the will of your Father: Matthew 18:14 NKJV

Where can I go from your Spirit: Psalm 139:7

Seek me and live: Amos 5:4

CHAPTER 4: "MY EYES FAIL, LOOKING FOR MY GOD" (PSALM 69:3)

I am worn out from groaning: Psalm 6:6
I have heard them crying out: Exodus 3:7–8
Pharaoh summoned Moses: Exodus 12:31–32
Then the whole congregation: Exodus 16:2 NKJV
What have I done to You: Job 7:20 NKJV
Now a certain man was sick: John 11:1 NKJV
I am willing. . . . Be clean: Matthew 8:3
Jesus loved Martha: John 11:5
So the sisters sent word to Jesus: John11:3
He stayed two more days: John 11:6 NKJV
This Mary: John 11:2
[Martha] went out to meet him: John 11:20
Hear, O LORD, and answer me: Psalm 86:1–2
Lord, if you had been here: John 11:32

CHAPTER 5: "NOT A SPARROW FALLS . . ." (MATTHEW 10:29 ADAPTED)

How precious also are Your thoughts to me: Psalm 139:17–18 NKJV
Precious in the sight of the LORD: Psalm 116:15
I have indeed seen the misery of my people: Exodus 3:7
Son of man, take up a lament: Ezekiel 27:2
I know the thoughts: Jeremiah 29:11 NKJV
My eyes fail from weeping: Lamentations 2:11

My heart is poured out on the ground: Lamentations 2:11

Sin entered the world: Romans 5:12

Surely He has borne our griefs: Isaiah 53:4 NKJV

CHAPTER 6: "BY HIS WOUNDS WE ARE HEALED" (ISAIAH 53:5)

His appearance was so disfigured: Isaiah 52:14

He poured out his life; The LORD has laid: Isaiah 53:12; Isaiah 53:6

I am poured out like water: Psalm 22:14

He was pierced; It was the LORD's will: Isaiah 53:5, 10

He was cut off from the land of the living: Isaiah 53:8

My God, my God, why have you forsaken me: Matthew 27:46

Behold! The Lamb of God: John 1:29 NKJV

The LORD makes His life a guilt offering: Isaiah 53:10

What shall I say: John 12:27

And when Jesus had cried out again: Matthew 27:50

CHAPTER 7: "BUT REJOICING COMES IN THE MORNING!" (PSALM 30:5)

Lazarus, come forth: John 11:43 NKJV

He has risen, just as He said: Matthew 28:6

Weeping may remain for a night: Psalm 30:5

The thief comes only to steal: John 10:10

I am the resurrection and the life: John 11:25

After three days: Matthew 27:63

118

Go quickly and tell His disciples: Matthew 28:7

Come to me. . . for I am gentle: Matthew 11:28–29

I will never leave you nor forsake you: Joshua 1:5

IN CLOSING: "LET US FIX OUR EYES ON JESUS" (HEBREWS 12:2)

And even the very hairs of your head: Matthew 10:30

I know the plans I have for you: Jeremiah 29:11

I am the bread of life: John 6:48

I have loved you with an everlasting love: Jeremiah 31:3

If you confess with your mouth: Romans 10:9

There will be more rejoicing in heaven: Luke 15:7

And God will wipe away every tear: Revelation 21:4 NKJV

And surely I am with you always: Matthew 28:20

Printed in the United States
By Bookmasters